Portofino

AF477424

St. Louis

Cuba
www.billbachmann.com

Cuzco

SEND ME ANYWHERE
BACHMANN ON LOCATION
Top of the World
Above the Arctic Circle

Serengeti

Iceland

Kathmandu

Jerusalem

South Africa

Bolestav Kvapil - FROM KAFKA'S DIARIES
Prague

Stonehenge

Brazil

Banff

Wyoming

Guilin

Vernazza, Cinque Terre

Las Vegas

South Africa

Mongolia

Rio de Janeiro

Pennsylvania

Angkor Wat

Bottom of the World

Paris

India

Santorini

Cambodia

All of my other books have stories and writing about the many photographs.

I wanted this book to be different!

My desire was for this book to be a tasty smorgasbord of brilliant colors from our Planet Earth. I wanted the colors and graphic perspectives of the images to speak to you without my words or interpretation.

The process of photography never is an automatic one. Most times in the morning I rarely have an idea what my film will look like in the evening. I just know that I put a lot of me into the effort. When I shoot people, I am looking for THAT MOMENT… that one instant where we create something that wasn't there before. Hopefully, I will endeavor to find a "soul" in my people pictures—some part of their being that I can record on film. That moment will never happen again.

When I look at pictures anywhere (whether they be mine in this book or another photographer's work) it is of great comfort to me when I realize that we all see the world creatively and differently. And I am often AMAZED at others photographers' work. I do hope that never stops happening to me when seeing images that I admire. What a joy it is to have photos that really touch others.

I did not choose to be a photographer—I HAD TO BE. I hope some of the images in this book have touched some inner part of you, as they have touched me…

Nova Scotia

Sydney

London

Laos

Siberia

Potala Palace

Bahamas

Carhenge, Nebraska

Arizona

Beijing

Venice

New Guinea

Florida

Uluru – Ayers Rock

Thailand

Outback Australia

Maine

Easter Island

Montana

St. Lucia

Tulum

Bora Bora

Normandy

Aruba

Mexico

Rome

Puerto Rico

Texas

Germany

Tibet

Guadeloupe

Monument Valley

Traveling has been one of the greatest blessings of my life. The places I have explored, the people I have met, the breath-taking vistas I have seen will be forever etched in my heart. I have so often stood in silent awe of God's creation of Earth.

I still find it so wonderful — and humbling — that people actually pay me to do what I love. I would never want a real job!

My camera often allows me to discover more about myself. When I travel, I often hide behind my camera and just watch life happen. I never really dislike traveling alone with cameras. People who don't know me would be surprised at that comment, but I find that traveling and shooting cleanses and refreshes some deep creative part of me.

The world is a book and those who do not travel really are reading only one chapter. There is so much wonder & joy out there to witness. I hope that I have inspired you to get your suitcase and head for some unknown place.

The true measure of success in life is not money, possessions or fame… it's laugh lines! So get out and enjoy this Earth we share. I promise you it is well worth it.

Greece

China

Bali

St. Vincent
& the Grenadines

Hawaii

Papua
New Guinea

Hanoi

Virgin Gorda

Tibet

Grenada

Budapest

Jamaica

New York

England

Havana

Dedication

This book is dedicated to four people in my family. First, to my wonderful parents—Ernest & Helen Bachmann—who raised me to develop a strong sense of WONDER. My Mom bought me my first Brownie camera at the age of four, and let me discover my childhood world taking pictures. She was a syndicated newspaper writer in Pittsburgh as I grew up, and she definitely taught me to think "outside of the box." Her love for photography & writing, her keen awareness of social causes, her integrity, and her idealistic persistency have been passed on in my blood, and I am forever thankful.

My father had a more gentle influence on my growth. His gentle spirit and ability to listen made the mysteries of childhood so much smoother. I so often remember sitting and talking to my Dad; his advice came almost invisibly as I silently incorporated his ideas into my decisions. He never showed me walls, only doors of opportunity. I will never be as good of a man as my father, but I will never stop striving. Dad is in heaven now, but I'll bet he often looks down to see what I'm photographing. I hope he's smiling...

I also dedicate this book to my two step-sons, Jordan Wilder and Brandon Wilder. I so luckily came into their lives as they were pre-teens, and I have changed for the better because of them. As teenagers, I helped them learn to drive, to shave, to play baseball, to become young men. I punished them when they were wrong, and also praised them when they did well. Having never been a parent, I sure learned as I went! I know that being their step-dad was a job that I took seriously and loved more than I could ever have imagined. I hope I helped them get through the bumps of childhood into manhood, as my Dad did for me.

I also hope there is another part of their life that I have influenced. I have guided both Jordan and Brandon as we experienced the world on trips. Hopefully, they have acquired an excitement & appreciation of travel. They have journeyed side-by-side with me into various countries, and I trust that they have come to love new cultures as much as I do. That would be my legacy to them—may they explore our wonderful planet with a sense of awe and respect. That would make me proud.

ISBN# 1-877659-05-3
Printed in the United States of America
1 2 3 4 5 6 7 8 9 10

Vietnam